Eric-Emmanuel Schmitt

Monsieur Ibrahim
and the Flowers of the Qur'an

Translated by Patricia Benecke and Patrick Driver

Methuen Drama

Published by Methuen Drama

1 3 5 7 9 10 8 6 4 2

First published in the UK in 2006 by
Methuen Publishing Limited

A CIP catalogue record for this book is available from
the British Library

ISBN 0 413 77590 9
978 0 413 77590 0

Typeset by Country Setting, Kingsdown, Kent

Caution

Dialogue Productions in association with
Guildford's Yvonne Arnaud Theatre, Richard Jordan and The Bush Theatre
present

monsieur IBRAHIM
and the Flowers of the Qur'an

by Eric-Emmanuel Schmitt
translated by Patricia Benecke and Patrick Driver
17 January – 11 February 2006

Cast

(In order of appearance)

Moses	**Ryan Sampson**
Monsieur Ibrahim	**Nadim Sawalha**

Director	**Patricia Benecke**
Designer	**Soutra Gilmour**
Lighting Designer	**John Harris**
Music	**Nikola Kodjabashia**
Assistant Director	**Patrick Driver**
Company Stage Manager	**Sarah Gentle**
Company Production Manager	**Guy Davey**
Education Officer	**Laura McFall**

Press Representation	**Alexandra Gammie** **020 7837 8333**
Marketing Consultant	**Paul Savident** **020 8567 2089**
Graphic Design	**Stem Design** **www.stemdesign.co.uk**

The Bush Ranger meets …
Ryan Sampson and Nadim Sawalha

The Bush Theatre's rove reporter caught up with the cast in rehearsals for *Monsieur Ibrahim and the Flowers of the Qur'an*.

'When this play came along I thought, "Yes, this is what I've been interested in all my life." ' Nadim Sawalha

Now that you're halfway through the rehearsal period, how is it all going?

Nadim Sawalha: We're two weeks in, and I feel comfortable that we're on target – we've got the moves in place, and most of the words too.

Ryan Sampson: Nadim's a bit more laid back than me as I panic at every juncture we come to. But that's what gets me through – I get worked up, and that moves me forward.

NS: Well, you're young and strong, and I'm old and weak. But that is the required temperament, so that's good. It is a play between a 13-year-old boy and a 70-year-old man, after all.

What attracted you both to the play when you first read it?

RS: I liked its unique style, the way that it chops and changes, and the way that it's pieced together. It isn't necessarily the choice of words used, but the way the scenes fall into place. We have to be quite innovative because there are only two of us in the cast, and it adds an exciting element of risk to it.

NS: I think that actors are in the business of acting to explore relationships, and this one seemed very interesting to me. First of all, because of the age difference: I'm a father and a grandfather, at the end of my family life so to speak. The new interest that arises between the Arab and the small Jewish boy is a relationship that seemed worth exploring. The interaction between faiths is also a wonderful topic, particularly nowadays, when there is an urge to understand one another's faiths and thus avoid the pitfalls of extremism. I liked the fact that neither aspect harangues the audience in this play: the interfaith discussions hang very loose; and the relationship is very sweet without being too saccharine.

*'We effectively reach out to the audience and say,
"I know you're there, and I'm talking to you right now" '*
Ryan Sampson

The bond between the two characters is really central to the play – how have you worked to create that?

RS: I think it's one of those things that you just let evolve. I'm sure that, when we're on stage, we will really be able to benefit from all the time we've spent together, and the preparation we've done. The comfort levels gained from being around each other throughout rehearsals will really be apparent.

NS: We have four to five weeks to rehearse, so it's a long journey of discovery. We began with the simple rule: 'Learn the lines and don't trip over the furniture'. Once that's established, we're able to start playing a little bit, to see where the two characters can gel together or draw away from each other.

The play itself has become a very famous story, performed all over the world and made into an award-winning film. Were you familiar with it before now?

RS: No, I didn't know of it. When I started asking people about it, however, it seemed that a lot of them knew of it already and I'd been missing out!

NS: I was aware of it before. Having lived all my life between two cultures, I have always been interested in this theme, which I call 'the bridge' in literature. I always grab any idea that tackles relationships between different faiths or nationalities. When this play came along I thought, "Yes, this is what I've been interested in all my life". If ever I've written anything, it's been about this bridge; if ever I've performed, it has mostly tackled the difference between cultures. So it was a very welcome idea to me.

The play relies a great deal on the imaginations of both actors and audience alike. How are you creating that world on stage?

RS: We ask the audience to just go with us, from the beginning of the play. From then on, we have given them a responsibility to suspend their disbelief, or to create for themselves the world that we are in. What they rely on, and need from us, are the little signifiers and gestures that show a mirror, for instance; or a different way of walking that shows we are on a beach. These interesting little intricacies can denote a whole world to the audience.

NS: I play a couple of ladies in the play, and what I have found very useful is to pretend to carry a handbag – only to create the character, of course. Once I have that, and start to hold my hands a certain way, I become that person. It just takes a little imaginary prop like that to lead me into the part. It can of course be discarded later but, in rehearsals, I like to carry that handbag.

RS: In one particular scene I get to play Brigitte Bardot, which is a lot of fun to do because I don't get many other characters to play. It's such a fun moment. There are a few scenes that stand alone, not contributing directly to the relationship between Momo and Monsieur Ibrahim, so we can really have a lot of fun with them. When Brigitte Bardot appears, it's just such a breath of fresh air as this completely different character, from a completely different world, walks in for just a second.

NS: It's tough because everybody has an idea of who Brigitte Bardot is, whereas the others are creations of the imagination, and not real people. It is a challenge, but that is what the actor does: he accepts the challenge, then jumps into the dark and hopes that he will land on his feet.

There's such a lively, humorous side to this play – are you having fun playing around with different ideas?

RS: In the beginning, it is just about playing with ideas, and it's been really important for this production. Every time we've messed around and experimented with something, it has been incredibly productive, and we've had a lot of fun with it.

NS: I think that sometimes the actor draws from his own life experiences and personal feelings. Whenever I ask myself how I would behave in this particular situation, I always find myself talking to one of my grandsons. He is a bit younger than the character of Momo, but he helps me to understand what I should be feeling, as Monsieur Ibrahim, towards the young stranger who comes into my shop.

RS: And I sometimes think about my grandmother. I think we have the same sort of reverence for her, in my family, which can be transposed onto my feelings for Monsieur Ibrahim. It really does help.

NS: So I'm your grandmother am I? I'll need another handbag...

How are you feeling about performing the play in the intimacy of The Bush theatre space?

RS: I came to see the current show at The Bush the other day, and I almost had a panic attack when I realised that the audience can see *everything*. You can see all of them too, as they are directly in front of your face. If there is someone in the audience that I know, I will see them and they will see me. It is a very strange feeling. We are actually quite lucky, because in this production we have to acknowledge the audience directly anyway. We effectively reach out to them and say, "I know you're there, and I'm talking to you right now; I'm not talking to a pretend audience or a friend, it's you".

NS: It was a frightening experience when I first performed at The Bush, about ten years ago. I remember coming onto the stage and just seeing hundreds of knees, almost up to my nose! I thought, "My god, I'm sitting on top of them!" But once you get used to it, the space is wonderful. I'm looking forward to seeing how differently I use the space now to when I first appeared there ten or fifteen years ago, as I've grown older and matured in so many ways since then. It is a magical space: I saw so many plays at The Bush during that period, as I was Chair of the Board, and each one transformed the stage. The designers do some incredible things, and I'm looking forward to seeing Soutra Gilmour's set for *Monsieur Ibrahim*.

RS: Our set is going to be quite sparse, because we have to be able to create so many different worlds from inside it. There are lots of different scenes that have to be created by the imagination, so the set has to be very easily changeable, and do anything that we want it to.

What do you hope audiences will take away with them from the play?

NS: I hope that audiences leave with the belief that being different is a source of joy, rather than a reason for conflict.

RS: And that it was a well spent 20 quid! Oh, not even that? – A mere £14!

19 Dec 05

Ryan Sampson Moses

Theatre includes *A Brief History of Helen of Troy* (Soho Theatre/UK tour), *Over Gardens Out* (Southwark Theatre), *Edward II* and *Richard III* (Crucible Theatre, Sheffield).

Television includes *In Denial Of Murder* and *Wire in the Blood*.

Nadim Sawalha
Monsieur Ibrahim

Theatre includes *All I Want is a British Passport* (Soho Theatre), *Homebody/Kabul* (Old Vic Theatre), *Turning Over* (Bush Theatre), *East is East*, *Jenkins Ear* (Royal Court), *The Waiting Room*, *Howard Katz*, *White Chameleon* (National Theatre), *A Dream of People* (RSC), *Waiting for Godot* (Lyric Theatre Studio, Hammersmith) and *Ousama – A Moslem Nobleman's View of the Crusades* (Shaw Theatre).

Television includes *If ... Cloning Could Cure Us*, *Close and True*, *Holby City*, *New Tricks*, *Moses and the Exodus*, *Mountbatten*, *Lovejoy*, *Big Battalions*, *Blue Heaven*, *Call Red*, *Expert Witness*, *Pirates*, *Inspector Morse*, *The Bill*, *Dangerfield*, *Justice in Wonderland*.

Film includes *The Spy Who Loved Me*, *The Living Daylights*, *The Avengers*, *The Wind and the Lion*, *A Touch of Class*, *Sinbad and the Eye of the Tiger*, *Pascali's Island*, *Half Moon Street*, *Son of the Pink Panther*, *Infinite Justice*, *Syriana*, *Arabian Nights* and *Cleopatra*.

Eric-Emmanuel Schmitt Writer

Within a decade, Eric-Emmanuel Schmitt has become one of the most read and acted French-language authors in the world.

Born in 1960, he was awarded a doctorate in Philosophy and a top teaching qualification. Schmitt first made a name for himself in the theatre with *The Visitor*, a play that posits a meeting between Freud and – possibly – God; the work soon became a classic and is now part of the international repertoire. Further successes quickly followed, including *Enigma Variations*, *The Libertine*, *Between Worlds*, *Partners in Crime*, *My Gospels* and *When Feelings Shift*. Acclaimed by audiences and critics alike, his works are now played in over 40 countries.

More recently, the four narratives (including *Monsieur Ibrahim and the Flowers of the Qur'an* and *Oscar and the Lady in Pink*) that make up his *Cycle de l'Invisible*, a series of tales dealing with childhood and spirituality, have met with huge international success both on the stage and in bookshops. His latest book *My Life with Mozart* is a strikingly original compilation of private correspondence with the Austrian composer. A keen music-lover, Eric-Emmanuel Schmitt has also translated into French *The Marriage of Figaro* and *Don Giovanni*.

www.eric-emmanuel-schmitt.com

Patricia Benecke Director

Patricia Benecke is joint Artistic Director of Dialogue Productions for which she directed *The MC Of A Striptease Act Doesn't Give Up*, *Heroes Like Us*, *Merlin* and *Top Dogs*.

Patricia works as a director in the UK and Germany. Previous repertory work in Germany includes *By the Bog of Cats* at Heilbronn Rep, and future work includes *Shining City* at Dortmund Rep.

She is associate director at the Horizont Theatre, Cologne, where her directing work includes: *Ghosts*, *Twilight of the Golds*, *The Fireraisers*, *The Transformed Comedian* (nominated for the Cologne Theatre Award) and *Far Away* (nominated for the Cologne Theatre Award).

Patricia is also a translator and the British theatre correspondent for Theater Heute and Neue Zürcher Zeitung.

Soutra Gilmour Designer

Theatre includes: *93.2* (Royal Court); *Saul, Hansel and Gretal* (Opera North); Mahler's *Ruckert Lieder* (Streetwise Opera); *A Brief History Of Helen Of Troy* (Soho Theatre and tour); *Hair* (Gate); *Shadow Of A Boy* (National Theatre); *Country Music* (Royal Court); *Ghost City* (59E59 New York); *When The World Was Green* (Young Vic); *Life Begins Season 04* (Liverpool Everyman); *Through The Leaves* (Southwark Playhouse, The Duchess, West End); *The Woman Who Swallowed A Pin* (Southwark Playhouse); *Therese Raquin* (Citizens' Theatre, Glasgow); *Hand In Hand* (Hampstead Theatre); *The Birthday Party* (Crucible, Sheffield); *Witness, Les Justes* (Gate) and *Tear From A Glass Eye* (Gate/National Studio).

Opera includes: *Mary Stuart* (English Touring Opera); *Girl of Sand* (Almeida); *El Cimmaron* (Queen Elizabeth Hall); *La Bohème* (Opera Ireland); *A Better Place* (English National Opera) and *Eight Songs for a Mad King* (National Theatre and world tour).

John Harris Lighting Designer

Recent credits include Associate Lighting Designer for *Miss Saigon* (UK Tour), Vari-Lite programmer for the Gala Performance of *Les Miserables* (Entente Cordiale, Windsor Castle, November 04) and as Lighting Designer of the world premiere of *Flying Under Bridges* (Watford Palace Theatre), *Kingfisher Blue* (The Bush Theatre), *Romeo and Juliet* (Birmingham Rep) and *Time's Up* (Yvonne Arnaud Theatre, Guildford).

As a Lighting Designer, theatre credits include: *Son of Man*, RSC; *Uncle Vanya*, Albery Theatre; *Michael Feinstein*, Comedy Theatre; *Women on The Verge of HRT*, UK Tour; *Small Change* and *Moving Susan* for the Basingstoke Haymarket. For the Arundel Festival, he has designed *Henry V, Macbeth* and *Midsummer Nights Dream* and *Much Ado About Nothing*. He has worked extensively for the Orange Tree in Richmond where his recent lighting designs include *The Road to the Sea, Simplicity, Me Myself and I, Dona Rosita Love's a Luxury'* (also at the Stephen Joseph Theatre) and *Myth Propaganda and Disaster....* For Guildford's Yvonne Arnaud Theatre he has designed *The Curious Quest for the Sandman's Sand, Skool & Crossbones, Shake Ripple & Roll, Pandemonium! (a Greek Myth-adventure)* including a run at the Edinburgh Festival 2001 and each pantomime since 2001. He was Chief Electrician at the Shaftesbury Theatre until 1995.

As a Vari-Lite programmer and crew chief he has worked around the world including Saudi Arabia, the Caribbean, Paris, Rome, Vienna, Athens and Dubai; as well as in the UK on the *Brit Awards*, Earls Court; the *MTV Awards*, Dublin; *Joy to the World*, Albert Hall; *Passion Play*, Donmar Warehouse and Comedy Theatre; *Hotstuff*, Leicester Haymarket; *Godspell*, for David Pugh; *The Buckingham Palace Jubliee Celebrations* for Unusual Events; *Torvill and Dean* at Nottingham's Ice Stadium; *Showtime at The Stadium* for BBC Wales & LSD at Cardiff's Millennium Stadium, the closing performance of *Cats* (London) for Cameron Mackintosh and as UK Moving Light Programmer for *The Producers* Theatre Royal Drury Lane.

Nikola Kodjabashia Music

Nikola Kodjabashia trained in Skopje, Bucharest, Romania, and with Sir Harrison Birtwistle at Kings College London.

Recent work includes an orchestral commission for *La Biennale di Musica Venezia*, music for the Olivier award-winning *Hecuba* (Donmar Warehouse); music for Kristijan Risteski's film *Remain Upstanding*; conductor and score editor on the soundtrack for *The Great Water*; composer and musical director of *The Birds* (National Theatre); musical director of Sir Peter Hall and Sir Harrison Birtwistle's *The Bacchae* (National Theatre, Newcastle Theatre Royal and Epidarus Festival, Greece).

Future work includes music for the stage production of Homer's *Odyssey*, commissioned by Northern Stage Theatre Company, Newcastle, and the score for the musical drama production of *Neuromancer* upon William Gibson's SF novel, with commissioned development by RPI, NY.

Nikola Kodjabashia's recordings are available at www.rermegacorp.com, www.meta4sounds.com and www.sjf.unet.com.mk

Patrick Driver Assistant Director

Patrick Driver is joint Artistic Director of Dialogue Productions and has performed in all their productions to date. He began his acting career at the Edinburgh Festival playing the title role in Howard Brenton's *Christie in Love*. Apart from his work for Dialogue Productions, Patrick's roles include Toby Belch in *Twelfth Night*, Dick Swiveller in *The Old Curiosity Shop*, both for Forest Forge, Milo Tindle in *Shaffer's Sleuth* at Eye Theatre, The Assassin in *Blondel* at St. Albans and the title role in *Pericles* for Wooden Tongues TC.

He worked for two years with the performance group OPTIK and in 1998, he joined Primitive Science and performed for them in *Hunger*, *Imperfect Librarian*, *Theatre Dream*, *Half Machine*, the award-winning *Icarus Falling* and *Poseidon* at the Young Vic. For the Royal Exchange, Manchester, Patrick has appeared in *Volpone* and *London Assurance*.

Television credits include: *Holby City*, *The Last Chancers*, *Peepshow*, *The Office*, *The Bill*, *Doctors*, *Grass*, *People Like Us*, *My Hero*, *Ghosts* and *Mr Charity*.

Laura McFall Education Officer

Laura McFall has a master's degree in Cross Sectoral and Community Arts from Goldsmiths College, London. She is currently a member of the advanced team of theatre educators at The National Theatre where projects include *Henry V*, *His Dark Materials*, *Slowtime*, *Greek Storytelling*, *Coram Boy* and *Pericles*. Other work includes running theatre projects for Art of Regeneration for The Albany Theatre Deptford, Group 64 Youth Theatre and Freshwater Theatre Company.

Beautiful Things

Alan Brodie
Anonymous
Barrie & Roxanne Wilson
Barry Serjent
Brian D Smith
Clive Butler
Clyde Cooper
David Brooks
David Hare
Jeremy Conway
John & Tita Shakeshaft
John Reynolds
Kate Brooke
Laurie Marsh
Matthew Byam Shaw
Michael McCoy
Mike Figgis
Mr & Mrs A Radcliffe
Mr and Mrs George
  Robinson
Sheila Hancock
Vivien Goodwin
William Keeling

Dialogue Productions Producer

Dialogue Productions is a London based Anglo-German theatre company. It was founded in 1996 with the aim of enhancing cultural dialogue between Great Britain and Germany by premiering the best contemporary German speaking drama in England. Subsequent projects have extended this remit to wider international work.

Key personnel are German director **Patricia Benecke** and British actor **Patrick Driver**. They find, translate and produce all company productions.

Company patrons are **Christoph Marthaler** and **Max Stafford-Clark**.

Productions to date:

1996 - 2003	Bodo Kirchhoff's *The MC of a Striptease Act Doesn't Give Up*, staged in London, Germany, Holland, Italy, Ireland, USA and at the Edinburgh Festival
1998	Urs Widmer's *Top Dogs*, presented as a site specific performance at The Truman Brewery in Brick Lane
2000	Thomas Brussig's *Heroes like Us*, in association with NXT, at The Edinburgh Festival
2001	Tankred Dorst's *Merlin*, the English premiere of this modern German classic, at the Riverside Studios Mainhouse
2003	*Top Dogs* revival at Southwark Playhouse
2005	*Top Dogs* national tour

This production of *Monsieur Ibrahim and the Flowers of the Qur'an* is supported by The Maurice et Noémi de Rothschild, Fondation pour l'Art.

Dialogue Productions would like to thank:

Baron and Baroness Benjamin de Rothschild, Firoz Ladak, Brian Kirk, Richard Jordan, John Cooper-Day, Justin Deaville, Zak Sawalha, Young Vic Theatre, Goethe-Institut London, Institut Français London and everyone at the Bush Theatre.

For more information: www.dialogueproductions.co.uk
Email: info@dialogueproductions.co.uk

Glee Club
Alan Rickman
Anonymous
Curtis Brown Group Ltd
Jim Broadbent

Handful of Stars
Gianni Alen-Buckley

Lone Star
Princess of Darkness

Bronze Corporate Membership
Act Productions Ltd
Anonymous

Silver Corporate Membership
The Agency (London) Ltd
Anonymous
Oberon Books Ltd

Platinum Corporate Membership
Anonymous

The Bush Theatre

The Bush Theatre opened in April 1972 in the upstairs dining room of The Bush Hotel, Shepherds Bush Green. The room had previously served as Lionel Blair's dance studio. Since then, The Bush has become the country's leading new writing venue with over 350 productions, premiering the finest new writing talent.

Playwrights whose works have been performed at The Bush include: Stephen Poliakoff, Robert Holman, Tina Brown, Snoo Wilson, John Byrne, Ron Hutchinson, Terry Johnson, Beth Henley, Kevin Elyot, Doug Lucie, Dusty Hughes, Sharman Macdonald, Billy Roche, Tony Kushner, Catherine Johnson, Philip Ridley, Richard Cameron, Jonathan Harvey, Richard Zajdlic, Naomi Wallace, David Eldridge, Conor McPherson, Joe Penhall, Helen Blakeman, Lucy Gannon, Mark O'Rowe and Charlotte Jones.

The theatre has also attracted major acting and directing talents including Bob Hoskins, Alan Rickman, Antony Sher, Stephen Rea, Frances Barber, Lindsay Duncan, Brian Cox, Kate Beckinsale, Patricia Hodge, Simon Callow, Alison Steadman, Jim Broadbent, Tim Roth, Jane Horrocks, Gwen Taylor, Mike Leigh, Mike Figgis, Mike Newell and Richard Wilson. Victoria Wood and Julie Walters first worked together at The Bush, and Victoria wrote her first sketch on an old typewriter she found backstage.

In over 30 years, The Bush has won over one hundred awards and recently received The Peggy Ramsay Foundation Project Award 2002. Bush plays, including most recently *The Glee Club*, have transferred to the West End. Off-Broadway transfers include *Howie the Rookie* and *Resident Alien*. Film adaptations include *Beautiful Thing* and *Disco Pigs*. Bush productions have toured throughout Britain, Europe, North America and Asia, most recently *Stitching, adrenalin... heart* (representing the UK in the Tokyo International Arts Festival, 2004) and *The Glee Club* (UK National Tour, Autumn 2004).

Every year The Bush receives over fifteen hundred scripts through the post, and reads them all.

According to The Sunday Times:

"What happens at The Bush today is at the very heart of tomorrow's theatre"

That's why we read all the scripts and will continue to do so.

Mike Bradwell
Artistic Director

Fiona Clark
Executive Producer

At The Bush Theatre

Artistic Director	**Mike Bradwell**
Executive Producer	**Fiona Clark**
Finance Manager	**Dave Smith**
Literary Manager	**Abigail Gonda**
Marketing Manager	**Nicki Marsh**
Production Manager	**Bob Holmes**
Theatre Administrator	**Nic Wass**
Chief Technician	**Sam Shortt**
Resident Stage Manager	**Ros Terry**
Administrative Assistant	**Lydia Fraser-Ward**
Box Office Supervisor	**Darren Elliott**
Box Office Assistants	**Rebecca Hartley** **Gail MacLeod**
Front of House Duty Managers	**Kellie Batchelor** **Adrian Christopher** **Lois Tucker** **Catherine Nix-Collins** **Sarah O'Neill**
Duty Technicians	**Graham Cutting** **Helen Spall** **Tom White**
Associate Artists	**Tanya Burns** **Es Devlin** **Paul Miller** **Richard Jordan**
Sheila Lemon Writer in Residence	**Jennifer Farmer**
Pearson Writer in Residence	**Steve Thompson**

The Bush Theatre
Shepherds Bush Green
London W12 8QD

VAT no. 228 3168 73

Be There At The Beginning

The Bush Theatre is a writer's theatre – dedicated to commissioning, developing and producing exclusively new plays. Up to seven writers each year are commissioned and we offer a bespoke programme of workshops and one-to-one dramaturgy to develop their plays. Our international reputation of over thirty years is built on consistently producing the very best work to the very highest standard.

With your help this work can continue to flourish.

The Bush Theatre's Patron Scheme delivers an exciting range of opportunities for individual and corporate giving, offering a closer relationship with the theatre and a wide range of benefits from ticket offers to special events. Above all, it is an ideal way to acknowledge your support for one of the world's greatest new writing theatres.

To join, please pick up an information pack from the foyer, call 020 7602 3703 or email info@bushtheatre.co.uk

We would like to thank our current members and invite you to join them!

Rookies

Alison Winter
Anonymous
Casarotto Ramsay & Associates Ltd
Clare Rich and Robert Marshall
Geraldine Caulfield
John & Jacqui Pearson
John Gowers
Lucy Heller
Mark Roberts
Martin Shenfield
Mr & Mrs Malcolm Ogden
Mr G Hopkinson
Ms Sian Hansen
Nina Drucker
Ray Miles
Ross Anderson
Tracey Scoffield

Monsieur Ibrahim
and the Flowers of the Qur'an

For Bruno Abraham-Kremer

Characters

Moses
Monsieur Ibrahim

The two actors taking the above parts play all other characters mentioned in the script.

Moses *comes on stage to Arabian music, listens, remembers, slowly starts to dance, to whirl like a Sufi dervish, enjoying it.*

His dance is interrupted by questions his invisible **Father** *shouts out.*

Father (*off*)   Moses, have you washed up?

Moses (*stops dancing*)   Yes, Father. (*Starts dancing again.*)

Father (*off*)   Moses, have you done the shopping?

Moses (*stops dancing*)   Yes, Father! (*Starts dancing again.*)

Father (*off*)   Moses, have you ironed my shirts?

Moses   Yes, Father!

He stops dancing altogether. Change of lighting. **Moses** *makes contact with the audience, addresses them directly, as he will for all following sections of narration.*

Moses   When I was eleven, I broke into my piggy-bank and went whoring. My piggy was made of puke-coloured china with a slot to let coins in but not out. My father had chosen that one-way piggy-bank because it met his philosophy: money should be saved and not spent.

There were two hundred francs inside the piggy. Four months' work. You see . . . one morning, four months earlier, while I was cleaning the flat before going to school, my father said –

Father *comes in.*

Father   Moses, I don't understand . . . there is money missing . . . From now on, you'll write down everything you spend on groceries on the notepad in the kitchen.

Moses   In other words, it wasn't enough being yelled at in school and at home, it wasn't enough cleaning up, studying, ironing, cooking, carrying the groceries or living alone in a dark, loveless flat, being the slave rather than the son of a no-client, no-wife lawyer, I also had to be taken for a thief!

As long as I was suspected of stealing, I might as well do it.

So, there were two hundred francs inside the piggy. That was the going rate for a girl on the rue du Paradis. That was the going rate for manhood.

He rehearses what he is going to say to the prostitutes in front of an imaginary mirror, trying to be as cool as possible, but really he is a little nervous.

'It's hot – do you want to go upstairs?' (*Different tones of voice.*)
'It's hot – do you want to go upstairs?' 'It's hot – how much?'

On the rue du Paradis

Moses   It's hot – do you want to go upstairs?

First Girl   Have you got any ID?

Moses   No – but I am sixteen! Honest!

First Girl   I don't think so, darling.

Moses (*as he walks away*)   Oh, there's a new girl!

He shows her the money. She smiles.

Second Girl   And you say you're sixteen?

Moses   Turned sixteen this morning.

Second Girl   Let's go upstairs, then.

Moses   I could hardly believe it – she was twenty-two, she was old and she was all mine. She told me how to wash myself, and then how to make love. Of course I already knew how, but I let her show me to make her feel better. All through it, I thought I was going to pass out.

Second Girl (*gently stroking his hair after they have finished*)   You have to come back and bring me a little present.

Moses   A little present! I ran back to the flat, I rushed into my room.

He looks frantically for a present, rejecting various items before settling on his teddy bear. He rushes back to the **Girl.**

Moses   Here is my present.

He hands his teddy to the **Girl**, *who is bemused, then touched.*

During **Moses**' *next lines,* **Monsieur Ibrahim** *sets up his shop.*

Moses   It was about the same time that I met Monsieur Ibrahim.

Every day I'd go shopping and cook meals. I only bought cans. I bought them daily, not because they'd be fresh, no, but because my father only left me a couple of coins in the morning.

When I started stealing from my father to punish him for suspecting me, I also started stealing from Monsieur Ibrahim.

Monsieur Ibrahim had always been old. As far back as anyone on the rue Bleue could remember, Monsieur Ibrahim had always tended his grocery shop; from eight a.m. till the middle of the night, he sat propped up between his till and the cleaning

fluids, one leg in the aisle, the other under the matchboxes,
a grey apron over his white shirt, with his ivory teeth under a
pencil-thin moustache, pistachio eyes, green and brown, lighter
than his brown, wisdom-spotted skin.

It was generally considered that Monsieur Ibrahim was a wise
man. Probably because for over forty years he'd been the
one Arab in a Jewish street. Probably because he smiled a lot
and said little. Probably because he seemed immune to the
restlessness of ordinary Parisians and never moved, like a
branch grafted onto his stool. He never replenished his displays
in front of anyone and disappeared between midnight and
eight a.m. – God knows where.

In **Monsieur Ibrahim***'s shop.*

Moses   In order to steal money from my father and yet feed
us both, I naturally had to steal from Monsieur Ibrahim. I felt
a little ashamed, but to conquer my shame, just as I was
paying, I'd think very hard:

'After all, he is only an Arab!'

Every day, I'd look straight into his eyes and give myself
courage.

'After all, he is only an Arab!'

Monsieur Ibrahim   I'm not an Arab, Momo, I'm from the
Golden Crescent.

Moses (*picks up his shopping, in shock*)   Monsieur Ibrahim could
hear me think! If he could hear me think, did that mean that
he knew I was stealing from him?

Moses   The next day I didn't steal any cans, but I asked:

'What is the Golden Cresent?'

Monsieur Ibrahim   It's the name of a region stretching from Anatolia to Persia, Momo.

Moses   The next day:

'My name isn't Momo, it's Moses.'

The next day:

Monsieur Ibrahim   I know your name is Moses, that's exactly why I call you Momo, it sounds less grand.

Moses   The next day:

'What do you care? Moses is Jewish, not Arab.'

Monsieur Ibrahim   I'm not an Arab, Momo, I'm a Muslim.

Moses   The next day.

'So why does everybody say you are the street's Arab when you're not an Arab?'

Monsieur Ibrahim   Arab means 'open at night and on Sundays' in the grocery business.

Moses   And such was our conversation. A sentence a day. We were in no hurry – he because he was old, I because I was young. And every other day, I'd steal a can from him.

I'm sure a one-hour conversation would have taken us a year or two, if we hadn't met Brigitte Bardot.

Moses   The rue Bleue is in turmoil. Traffic is being stopped. A film is being shot.

Monsieur Ibrahim *and* **Moses** *create an excited atmosphere, run about, become other characters on the street gasping, whispering, whistling, trying to catch a glimpse of* **Brigitte Bardot**.

Moses   Brigitte Bardot is there, in the flesh. I positioned myself at our window. (*A beat. Dumbfounded.*) Monsieur Ibrahim was standing outside, on his doorstep. For the first time ever – at least to my knowledge – he'd left his stool. I decided to take advantage of his momentary lapse of attention and steal several cans from him. – Disaster! Monsieur Ibrahim was back behind his till. But his eyes were laughing and peering over his soap bars and clothes pegs to observe the film star. I'd never seen him like this.

'Monsieur Ibrahim, are you married?'

Monsieur Ibrahim (*surprised – he isn't used to people asking him questions*)   Of course I am married.

Moses   I thought all you had in life was your shop.

Monsieur Ibrahim (*keeps looking out, his eyes laughing*)   I'm imagining I'm in a boat with my wife and Brigitte Bardot. My boat is sinking. You know what I'd do?

Moses   What?

Monsieur Ibrahim   I'd bet my wife can swim.

They laugh together.

Suddenly, all decks are cleared for action, **Monsieur Ibrahim** *stands to attention:* **Brigitte Bardot** *enters his store.*

Monsieur Ibrahim   Bonjour, Mademoiselle Bardot.

Brigitte Bardot   Bonjour, Monsieur, do you have water?

Monsieur Ibrahim   Of course, Mademoiselle.

He gets up from his stool, gets a bottle of water from the shelf and brings it to her himself.

Brigitte Bardot   Merci, Monsieur. How much is it?

Monsieur Ibrahim   Forty francs, Mademoiselle.

Brigitte Bardot *flinches, purses her lips.*

Brigitte Bardot   Forty francs? I didn't realise water was so scarce around here.

Monsieur Ibrahim   It isn't water that is scarce, Mademoiselle, but stars.

Moses   He said it with such charm, such an irresistible smile, that Brigitte Bardot blushed a little, handed him forty francs and left.

'You've got some chutzpah, Monsieur Ibrahim.'

Monsieur Ibrahim   Well, you see, my little Momo, somehow I have to make back the money for all the cans you've nicked from me.

Moses, *mortally embarrassed, wants to leave the shop quickly.*

Monsieur Ibrahim (*smiling*)   Momo, don't worry about it.

Moses   I'm going to pay you back.

Monsieur Ibrahim   You owe me nothing – do you hear me, Momo? – nothing. And if you want to steal, then only from me – swear.

Moses   I swear.

Monsieur Ibrahim   Do you know what you're going to cook for your father tonight?

Moses *shakes his head.*

Monsieur Ibrahim (*picking the different ingredients from his shelf*)
Well, if you want to save money and you don't want him to
notice, try serving him stale bread after you've baked it a little
in the oven!

Moses   Oh!

Monsieur Ibrahim   And gradually add chicory to his
coffee-powder!

Moses   Okay!

Monsieur Ibrahim   Mix his usual Beaujolais with cheap
three-franc wine . . .

Moses (*getting into it*)   And recycle his tea bags!

They laugh.

But the best idea, the one to top them all, the one that proved
Monsieur Ibrahim was a master of the art:

Monsieur Ibrahim   Replace his liver pâté with dog food.

Moses   Thanks to Monsieur Ibrahim's intervention, the
world of grown-ups cracked open; it was no longer the same,
impenetrable wall I used to knock my head against. A hand
was reaching out to me through the crack.

And I had saved up two hundred francs again. (*He winks.*)

Monsieur Ibrahim and the whores were making my life with
my father even more difficult. For I'd started doing something
both dreadful and dizzying. Making comparisons. With
Monsieur Ibrahim and the girls, I felt warm, light. With my
father, I was always cold.

Moses' *flat.*

Moses (*to* **Father**)   So these books are supposed to contain all the achievements of the human mind?

Father   Shut the blinds, Moses, the light ruins the bindings.

He sits and reads in his armchair, paying no attention to **Moses.**

Moses   He didn't pay any more attention to me than he would to a dog – and he hated dogs. He wasn't even inclined to throw me a scrap of his knowledge.

Moses *moves a little noisily; the* **Father** *twitches as if* **Moses** *was a mosquito.* **Moses** *hums; his* **Father** *sighs heavily.*

Moses   Sorry . . .

Father   Quiet, Moses. I'm reading. I'm working.

Moses   Sorry.

Father   Be quiet! Thank goodness your brother Popol wasn't like this.

Moses   My older brother Popol was another name for my inadequacy.

Father (*while* **Moses** *quietly mouthes his words – he has heard it all before*)   Popol studied very hard. Popol loved maths. Popol never left the bath dirty. Popol never peed next to the bowl. Popol loved reading his dad's books.

Moses   Maybe it wasn't so bad after all that my mother had left with Popol soon after my birth. If it was already impossible to live up to a memory, how would I have coped with perfection in the flesh?

'Dad, what do you think, would Popol have liked me?'

Father (*stares at* **Moses**, *bewildered*)   What kind of question is that?

Moses   'What kind of question is that?' – That was my answer.

Monsieur Ibrahim's *shop.*

Monsieur Ibrahim   Momo, why don't you ever smile?

Moses   Smiling is for rich people. I can't afford it.

Monsieur Ibrahim (*smiling, to tease* **Moses**)   So you think I'm rich?

Moses   I don't know anybody else who sees such a lot of cash all day long.

Monsieur Ibrahim   But I use that cash to pay for the stock and the rent. At the end of the month, there isn't all that much left, you know.

An even broader smile to tease **Moses** *some more.*

Moses   Monsieur Ibrahim, when I say smiling is just for rich people, I meant it's just for happy people.

Monsieur Ibrahim   Well, that's where you're wrong. It's the smiling that makes you happy, not the other way round.

Moses   Rubbish.

Monsieur Ibrahim   Try it.

Moses   Rubbish.

Monsieur Ibrahim   Are you polite, Momo?

Moses   Have to be, otherwise I get a slap round the chops.

Monsieur Ibrahim   Being polite is good. Being friendly is better. Try a smile, and you'll see.

Moses   Okay then, whatever, if I'm being asked so nicely by Monsieur Ibrahim, who slips me a can of superior sauerkraut, I'll try it . . .

The next day, I really behave as if I'd seen the light: I'm smiling at all and sundry.

At **Moses'** *school*

Moses   In class:

'I'm sorry, Madame, I didn't understand the math problem.'

Bang: smile!

'I just couldn't solve it.'

Teacher   All right, Moses, I'll explain it again.

Moses   Never experienced that in my life. No shouting, no warning. Nothing.

In the school canteen:

'Could I have some extra vanilla custard?'

Bang: smile!

Chef   There you are, now.

Moses   In the gym:

Teacher   Who is the one with the smelly trainers?

Moses   'I think I am, sir. Sorry.'

Bang: smile!

Teacher *laughs and pats* **Moses** *on the shoulder.*

Moses   Exhilarating! No one can resist me. Monsieur Ibrahim has given me the most potent of weapons. I bombard the whole world with my smile. And I am no longer treated like a cockroach.

Moses   That night, when my father got home, I helped him to take off his coat as usual, then I stood in front of him in the light to make sure that he could see me.

'Dinner's ready.'

Bang: smile!

Father *looks at* **Moses,** *amazed.* **Moses** *carries on smiling, slightly strained.*

Father   Have you done something stupid?

Moses' *smile vanishes instantly.*

Moses   But I wasn't discouraged. When I served him dessert, I tried again

He smiles. **Father** *looks at him, uncomfortable.*

Father   Come here.

Moses   I knew my smile was winning him over. Maybe he wanted to give me a kiss?

Father (*looking carefully at* **Moses**)   You're going to have to wear braces. I never noticed you had buck teeth.

Monsieur Ibrahim's *shop.*

Moses   That evening, I started visiting Monsieur Ibrahim at night, as soon as my father was asleep.

'It's my fault. If I was like Popol, my father would find it easier to love me.'

Monsieur Ibrahim   How do you know? Popol is gone.

Moses   And? So?

Monsieur Ibrahim   So maybe he couldn't stand your father any longer.

Moses   You think so?

Monsieur Ibrahim   He has left. That's proof enough for me. Here, can you count this for me? It calms the nerves.

He gives **Moses** *change to count.*

Moses   Monsieur Ibrahim, you knew Popol, didn't you?

Monsieur Ibrahim *doesn't answer.*

Moses   What did you think of Popol?

Monsieur Ibrahim *sighs, looks at the ceiling, then slams his till as though to prevent it from speaking.*

Monsieur Ibrahim   Momo, let me tell you one thing: I like you a hundred, a thousand times more than Popol.

Moses   You do?

He is happy, but does't want to show it. He clenches his fists and bares his teeth a little, ready to defend his family.

But I won't let you bad-mouth my brother. What did you have against Popol?

Monsieur Ibrahim (*sees danger coming and gets careful*)   He was nice, Popol, very nice. But, I'm sorry, I like Momo better.

Beat.

Moses   My father says I need braces.

Monsieur Ibrahim   Just don't smile so much, that'll do – (*Beat.*) Momo, that's a joke!

Can you picture yourself with braces on the rue de Paradis? Which one would believe you're sixteen then?

He has hit a nerve.

Moses (*to regain composure*)   Can I count some more change? (*Beat.*) Monsieur Ibrahim, how do you know about me and the girls on . . . ?

Monsieur Ibrahim   I don't know anything. I just know what's in my Qur'an.

Moses (*still counting change*)   Do you sometimes go to the rue de Paradis?

Monsieur Ibrahim   Paradise is for everyone.

Moses   Now, you're having me on. Don't tell me you still go there, at your age!

Monsieur Ibrahim (*shooting* **Moses** *a withering look*)   Why not? Is it reserved for under-age kids?

Pause.

Momo, what do you think about going for a walk with me?

Moses   Really, do you walk sometimes, Monsieur Ibrahim?

He realises this is another faux pas, and uses his magic weapon − a big smile.

What I mean is, I've only ever seen you sitting on that stool.

The following day, **Monsieur Ibrahim** *shows* **Moses** *Paris.*

Moses   So this is Paris! The Paris that's pretty, the one in the pictures, the Paris of tourists.

Monsieur Ibrahim *and* **Moses** *see the sights − from the Eiffel Tower.*

Monsieur Ibrahim   There, the Seine!

Moses   The Champs Elysées!

Monsieur Ibrahim   The rue Faubourg Saint-Honoré − where we were walking a moment ago, remember?

Moses   The one with all the famous brand names: Hermès, Saint-Laurent, Cardin . . . Funny, those huge empty shops compared to yours which is no bigger than a bathroom, but has indispensable things stacked from floor to ceiling. Isn't it strange how poor the windows of the rich are? There's nothing in them.

Monsieur Ibrahim   Well, that's luxury, Momo, nothing in the window, nothing in the shop, everything in the price. Have some lemonade.

Moses   In the garden of the Palais Royal, Monsieur Ibrahim regained his legendary immobile stance on a bar stool.

'Must be nice, living in Paris.'

Monsieur Ibrahim   You do live in Paris, Momo.

Moses   No, I don't. I live on the rue Bleue.

Monsieur Ibrahim *sips his aperitif.* **Moses** *watches him.*

Moses   I thought Muslims didn't drink alcohol.

Monsieur Ibrahim   That's right. But I'm a Sufi.

Moses   I realised I was being nosy. If Monsieur Ibrahim didn't want to tell me anything else about his disease, that was his privilege, and I kept silent until we got back home.

In **Moses**' *flat.*

Moses *takes a dictionary from his* **Father**'s *books. Looks for the right entry.*

Moses (*reads to himself*)   'Su . . . Su . . . Sufism: school of
Islam, originated in the eighth century. It opposes legalism and
stresses inner contemplation.' Well, the one important thing is
that Sufism isn't a disease, that's quite reassuring, it's a way of
thinking – although there also are ways of thinking which are
a disease, Monsieur Ibrahim says.

During this speech, **Moses** *prepares dinner from dog-food tins.*

After that, I tried to understand all the words in the definition.
It transpired that Monsieur Ibrahim with his aperitif believed
in God the Muslim way, but in a way that almost verged on
illegality, 'opposed to legalism' – that one really puzzled me . . .
If legalism really means 'strict, literal or excessive conformity
to the law', as these dictionary people claimed, on the whole
it means something pretty bad – that Monsieur Ibrahim was
dishonest, and that I associated with people I shouldn't
associate with. But at the same time, if conforming with the
law meant being a lawyer like my father, with his grey face,
having about as much conversation as a toilet bowl, spreading
sadness at home, I'd rather be against legalism with Monsieur
Ibrahim. And the dictionary people added that Sufism had
been thought up by two old guys, Al-Halladj and Al-Ghazali.
People with names like that could only live in tiny top-floor
rooms in the backyard – on the rue Bleue, anyway. As for the
inner contemplation, that made sense – Monsieur Ibrahim
really didn't say much compared to all the Jews on the street.

Moses *and his* **Father** *are having dinner.*

Moses   Do you like your lamb stew?

Father *nods.*

Moses   Dad, do you believe in God?

Father (*looks at* **Moses,** *then says slowly*)   I see you're becoming a man.

Moses *looks at him, bewildered, can't see the connection.*

Father   No, I've never managed to believe in God.

Moses   Never managed? Why? Do you have to make such an effort?

Father (*looking around in the half-dark flat*)   To believe that all of this has a meaning? Yes. You have to make a tremendous effort.

Moses   But we're Jews, Dad, you and me?

Father   Yes.

Moses   And being a Jew has nothing to do with God?

Father   Not any more. For me, being a Jew only means having memories. Bad memories. (*He looks as if he is in pain.*)

Moses   Do you need an Aspirin?

Father *gets up without a word and leaves the table.*

Moses   A few days later he came back, looking even paler than usual. I started feeling guilty. I told myself that I'd ruined his health with all the dog food I gave him to eat.

Father *sits down and motions* **Moses** *over. Wants to say something but takes ages before he gets a word out.*

Father   I was fired, Moses. The firm I work for doesn't want me any more. I'm going to have to find another job. Somewhere else. I don't know what. We'll have to tighten our belts.

Moses   To be honest, it didn't surprise me much that people wouldn't want to work with my father – he must have depressed the hell out of the criminals. At the same time, I'd never imagined a lawyer could stop being a lawyer. He went to bed. He obviously didn't care in the slightest how I felt about the whole thing.

He goes to **Monsieur Ibrahim,** *who is munching some peanuts, smiling.*

Moses   How do you manage to be so happy, Monsieur Ibrahim?

Monsieur Ibrahim   I know what's in my Qur'an.

Moses   Maybe I should nick your Qur'an someday. But that's not allowed when you're a Jew.

Monsieur Ibrahim   Hmm . . . what does it mean to you, Momo, being a Jew?

Moses   Don't know. For my father, it means being depressed all day long. For me . . . it's just something which doesn't allow me to be anything else.

Monsieur Ibrahim *offers* **Moses** *a peanut.*

Monsieur Ibrahim   Your shoes are falling apart. Tomorrow, we'll buy you a new pair.

Moses   Yes, but . . .

Monsieur Ibrahim   A man spends his life only in two places: his bed or his shoes.

Moses   I've got no money, Monsieur Ibrahim.

Monsieur Ibrahim   I will pay for them. A present. You only have one pair of feet: if your shoes hurt, change them – you can never change your feet.

Moses   The following day, when I came back from school, I found a note on the floor of our dark hall. (*He looks at the paper. Recognises worriedly:*) That's my father's handwriting.

> 'Moses,
>   I am sorry, but I'm leaving. I simply don't have it in me to be a father.
>   Popo . . . '

That's crossed out. He probably wanted to say something about Popol like, 'With Popol, I could have made it, with you, I can't,' or, 'Popol would have given me the strength and energy to be a father, you don't,' or something of that ilk he didn't dare to write down in the end. Well, you didn't have to write it. I got the message, thanks very much.

> 'Maybe we'll meet again someday, when you're grown up. When I don't feel quite so ashamed and when you've found it in you to forgive me. Farewell.'

Farewell, exactly!

> 'P.S. What money I have left is on the table. Here is a list of people who need to know I'm gone. They'll take care of you.'

And then a list of four names I'd never heard.

I took a decision. I had to pretend.

No way would I admit to being abandoned, that was out of the question. Abandoned twice: once by my mother when I was born; a second time by my father when I was a teenager. If word got around, no one would give me the time of day. What was so repulsive about me? What did I have that made it impossible to love me?

My decision was irrevocable: I'd fake my father's presence. I'd make everyone think he still lived here, ate here, shared his long, tedious evenings with me.

So I didn't hesitate another second: I went down to the shop.

'Monsieur Ibrahim, my father has stomach problems. What should I give him?'

Monsieur Ibrahim   Alka-Seltzer, Momo. Here's a box.

Moses   Thanks. I'm going straight back up to give them to him.

Monsieur Ibrahim   Wait a second, Momo.

He gets out a brand new book and hands it to **Moses**.

Moses   A Qur'an?!

Monsieur Ibrahim (*smiles*)   Off you go!

Moses   The money my father left me lasted a month. I learned to forge his signature to fill in the necessary forms, to answer letters from school. I kept cooking for both of us, served dinner for two each night; only that I threw his portion into the bin.

A few nights a week, for the benefit of the neighbours across the street, I sat in his chair with his pullover, his shoes, flour in my hair, and tried to read my beautiful, brand new Qur'an.

I had to prove to myself that I was lovable. I told myself that at school there was no time to lose: I had to fall in love. There wasn't much of a choice given that it was a boys' school; everyone was in love with the caretaker's daughter, Myriam. Although she was only thirteen, she had twigged she was ruling over three hundred panting pubescent boys. I started courting her with the ardour of a drowning man.

Bang: smile!

Someone had to love me before the whole world discovered that even my parents, the only ones who had a duty to love me, had cleared off.

Monsieur Ibrahim   And how is your father? I don't see him any more . . .

Moses   He works long hours. He has to leave really early with his new job.

Monsieur Ibrahim   Is that so? And isn't he upset you're reading the Qur'an?

Moses   I'm doing it secretly . . . and besides, I don't really get what it says.

Monsieur Ibrahim   To learn something, you don't pick up a book. You find people you can speak with. I don't believe in books.

Moses   But you always tell me, Monsieur Ibrahim, that you know what's . . .

Monsieur Ibrahim   Yes, that I know what's in my Qur'an . . . Momo, I feel like going to Normandy. Would you like to come?

Moses   Really?

Monsieur Ibrahim   Only if it's all right with your father, of course.

Moses   It will be.

Monsieur Ibrahim   Are you sure?

Moses   I'm telling you it will!

Monsieur Ibrahim *and* **Moses** *arrive in the lobby of Cabourg's Grand Hotel.* **Moses** *can't help it: he starts to cry. He cries for a long time.* **Monsieur Ibrahim** *watches and waits patiently for* **Moses** *to say something.* **Moses** *finally manages to get out a few words.*

Moses   This is too beautiful, Monsieur Ibrahim, far too beautiful. It's not for me. I don't deserve it.

Monsieur Ibrahim (*smiles*)   Beauty is everywhere. No matter where you turn your eye, Momo. That's in my Qur'an.

Moses   In the days which followed, we walked along the beach and I told him about Myriam. I wanted to avoid the subject of my father, so I talked about her a lot.

'First she admits me among her flock of suitors – and then she rejects me as unworthy of her.'

Monsieur Ibrahim   That doesn't matter a bit. Your love for her belongs to you. No one can take it from you. Even if she doesn't want it, she can't change it. She's missing out on something, that's all. What you give away is yours for ever, Momo, what you hold on to is for ever lost!

Moses   But you've got a wife?

Monsieur Ibrahim   Yes.

Moses   And why isn't she here with you?

Monsieur Ibrahim (*pointing at the sea*)   This really is an English sea, all grey and green. These aren't normal watercolours. It looks almost as if it had picked up the accent.

Moses   You didn't answer my question about your wife, Monsieur Ibrahim.

Monsieur Ibrahim   Momo, no answer is an answer.

Moses   Every morning, Monsieur Ibrahim was the first one up. He would stand by the window, sniff the light and do his exercises. He was amazingly limber and, from where I was lying in my bed, I could still see with my eyes half-open the slow, laid-back young man he'd probably been way back.

Monsieur Ibrahim *and* **Moses** *are in the bathroom together.*

Moses (*amazed*)   You, too, Monsieur Ibrahim?!

Monsieur Ibrahim   Muslims are circumcised just like Jews, Momo. It's Abraham's sacrifice: he reaches out to God by offering him his child. That little bit of skin missing is the mark of Abraham. During circumcision, the father has to hold his son – the father offers his own pain up as a memory to Abraham's sacrifice.

Moses   Monsieur Ibrahim made me realise how Jews, Muslims and even Christians had plenty of great men in common before they started hitting each other on the head. None of my business, of course, but it made me feel good, somehow.

Moses   When we returned from Normandy, I walked back into the dark, empty apartment. I didn't feel any different, but I thought the world could be different. I could open up the windows, the walls could be lighter. Maybe I didn't have to keep the furniture that smelled of the past. Not a particularly beautiful past, no, a past which stank like an old dishcloth.

I didn't have any money left. I started out by selling the books, piles of them, to the booksellers by the Seine. With every book sold I felt little freer.

Three months had passed since my father had gone. I still pretended to cook for two and, strangely enough, Monsieur Ibrahim questioned me less and less about him. My relationship with Myriam worsened by the minute, but it still made for great nightly conversation with Monsieur Ibrahim.

True, I did feel sad on certain nights. Because I thought about Popol. With my father gone, I wished I'd known Popol. I was sure I could have tolerated him better now that he wasn't constantly thrown in my face to illustrate my uselessness. I often went to bed thinking that, somewhere in the world, I had a beautiful, perfect brother. I didn't know him, but maybe someday I'd meet him.

A loud knock on the door.

Policeman (*shouting from off*)   Police! Open up!

Moses   This is it! I'm in deep shit, I lied too much, they're going to arrest me.

He cautiously unlocks the door.

Policeman (*to* **Moses***' surprise, politely*)   Can I come in?

He steps in. Takes **Moses***' hand, with a friendly tone.*

Policeman   I have some bad news for you, son. Your father is dead.

Moses   I couldn't say what surprised me most: my father being dead or the policeman calling me 'son'.

Policeman   He threw himself under a train in Marseilles.

Moses (*bewildered*)   Why go to Marseilles for that! There are plenty of trains everywhere. There are more trains in Paris than in Marseilles. Really, I'll never understand my father.

Policeman   There is every reason to believe your father was desperate and voluntarily ended his life.

Silence. **Policeman** *glances around the room.*

Is there anybody we should tell?

Moses (*gets the list of names his* **Father** *left*)   A list of names he left me.

Policeman *steps towards* **Moses** *with a sad face.* **Moses** *can tell something is up.*

Moses   You're going to ask me something weird, aren't you.

Policeman   I have to ask you something difficult now: you will have to identify the body.

That is like an alarm signal. **Moses** *starts howling as if someone had pushed a button. The* **Policeman** *hovers around him as though looking for a switch. But* **Moses** *can't stop.*

Moses (*cries*)   Monsieur Ibrahim! Monsieur Ibrahim!!

Quick transition: **Policeman** *becomes* **Monsieur Ibrahim.**

Monsieur Ibrahim   Stop crying, Momo, I'll go to Marseille to identify the body.

Moses   At first, the policeman didn't trust him because he was an Arab, but when I started howling again, he accepted Monsieur Ibrahim's offer.

After the funeral.

Moses   How long ago did you know, Monsieur Ibrahim?

Monsieur Ibrahim   Since Normandy. But you shouldn't be angry with your father, you know.

Moses   Really? Why not? A father who tells me I stink, who abandons me and then kills himself – that's very likely to make me trust in life. And I'm not supposed be angry with him?

Monsieur Ibrahim   Your father had no example to follow. He lost his parents when he was very young; they were carted away by the Nazis and died in camps. Your father never got over escaping their fate. He blamed himself for surviving. It's no accident he died under the wheels of a train.

Moses   Why?

Monsieur Ibrahim   His parents had to take a train to their death. Maybe he'd always been looking for his train. If he didn't have the strength to carry on living, it wasn't because of you, but because of what happened or didn't happen before you.

Moses   I started changing everything in the rue Bleue apartment. Monsieur Ibrahim gave me some cans of paint and some brushes. He also gave me some tips on how to drive the social worker insane to gain time.

One afternoon I was opening up all the windows in the apartment to chase away the smell of paint when a woman walked in.

I knew instantly who she was.

The **Woman** *is embarrassed. She hesitates, then gingerly steps between the ladders.* **Moses** *pretends he is deeply immersed in his work.*

The **Woman** *softly clears her throat.*

Moses (*feigning surprise*)   Are you looking for someone?

Woman   I'm looking for Moses.

Moses (*enjoying leading her on*)   Who are you?

Woman   I'm his mother.

The **Woman** *looks at* **Moses** *intently, trying to read his features. She looks frightened.*

Woman   And you, who are you?

Moses   Me? – Everyone calls me Momo.

The **Woman***'s face collapses.*

Moses (*grinning*)   It's short for Mohammed.

The **Woman** *grows even paler.*

Woman   What? You're not Moses?

Moses   Oh no. Don't get confused, Madame. I'm Mohammed.

The **Woman** *sighs, is maybe even slightly relieved.*

Woman   But isn't there a boy living here who's called Moses?

Moses (*quietly to himself*)   I don't know. You're his mother, you're the one who ought to know. (*Aloud.*) Moses is gone, He'd had enough of being here, he didn't have any happy memories here.

Woman   Didn't he?

She doesn't seem convinced, looks as if she may not believe him, after all. She keeps on staring at him.

When is he coming back?

Moses   I don't know. When he left he said he was going to see his brother.

Woman   His brother?

Moses   Yes, Moses has a brother.

Woman   Does he?

She is totally nonplussed. She holds on to a ladder for support.

Moses   Yes, his brother Popol.

Woman   Popol?

Moses   Popol, his older brother!

Woman   But Moses was my first child. I never had a child named Popol.

Now it's **Moses** *who is feeling faint. They both need to sit down in an armchair to catch their breath. They stare at each othe. She searches his face.*

Woman   Tell me, Momo . . .

Moses   Mohammed.

Woman   Tell me, Mohammed, is there a chance you might see Moses again?

Moses (*trying to sound as casual as possible*)   Maybe.

Woman   If you ever see Moses again, tell him I was very young when I married his father -- I only married him so I could leave home. I never loved Moses' father. But I was ready to love Moses. Only I met another man. I studied to become a lawyer myself. Your father . . .

Moses   Pardon?

Woman   His father, Moses' father, said: 'Go, but leave me Moses, or else . . . ' I left. I chose to build a new life for myself. A life in which there was, and is, happiness.

Moses   Sounds good.

The **Woman** *lowers her eyes. She steps towards him. It looks as if she might kiss* **Moses**. *He pretends not to understand.*

Woman   You will tell Moses, won't you?

Moses   I might.

Moses   That same evening, I went to see Monsieur Ibrahim and asked him jokingly:

'So, when are you going to adopt me?'

Monsieur Ibrahim (*as jokingly*)   How about tomorrow if that's okay with you, my little Momo?

Moses   We had to fight. The official world, the world of stamps, of approvals, of clerks who resent being woken from their sleep, didn't want to hear about us. But nothing discouraged Monsieur Ibrahim.

Monsieur Ibrahim   We already have a 'No' in our pockets. Now let's go and get a 'Yes'.

Moses   My mother has finally agreed to it! And how about your wife, Monsieur Ibrahim, is she all right with it?

Monsieur Ibrahim   My wife went back to our country a long time ago. I can do whatever I want. But if you wish, we can visit her next summer.

Moses   On the day we received the paper, the paper that said that from now on, I was the son of the man I had chosen, Monsieur Ibrahim said:

Monsieur Ibrahim   Let's buy a car to celebrate, Momo! We'll go travelling together. And next summer, we'll go to the Golden Crescent. I'll show you the sea, the one and only sea, the sea from which I come.

Moses   Couldn't we go there on a flying carpet?

Monsieur Ibrahim   Carpets fly too low these days. Why don't you take a look at the catalogues and choose a car instead?

Moses   Yes, Dad.

Amazing how, with the exact same words, you can have such different feelings. Whenever I called my father 'Dad', it felt like a tedious duty. When I called Monsieur Ibrahim 'Dad', my heart was laughing, and the future seemed bright. And Monsieur Ibrahim was even worse than I as far as vocabulary was concerned. He ended each sentence with 'my son', as though he'd just invented fatherhood.

At the car dealership.

Monsieur Ibrahim   I want to buy this one. My son picked it.

Salesman   Very good choice, sir; this model has an automatic –

Monsieur Ibrahim   You don't have to give me a song and dance about it, I'm telling you I want to buy it.

Salesman   Do you have a driving licence?

Monsieur Ibrahim   A driving licence ? Of course I have.

He takes out his leather wallet and pulls from it a document that looks like it dates back to the Pyramids. The salesman examines the papyrus with a frightened look – on the one hand, because most of the writing is erased, on the other, because it is in a language he doesn't understand.

Salesman   That's a driving licence?

Monsieur Ibrahim (*indignantly*)   Can't you tell?

Salesman   Fine. You have the option of paying in instalments. Over a period of three years, for example, you would . . .

Monsieur Ibrahim (*deeply offended*)   When I say I want to buy a car, it means I can. I want to pay cash.

The **Salesman** *gets flustered as he seems to put his foot in it whenever he opens his mouth.*

Salesman   In this case would you please write us a cheque for . . .

Monsieur Ibrahim   Enough is enough! I'm telling you I'm paying cash. With money. Real money.

He puts down wads of banknotes on the table, all nice and tidy, taking them out of plastic bags. The salesman gasps.

Salesman   But . . . but . . . no one ever pays cash . . . that's . . . that's just not done.

Monsieur Ibrahim   Well, are you going to tell me this isn't money? I've accepted it from customers, so why can't you? Momo, what kind of establishment is this, huh?

Salesman   All right then. Let's move on. We'll deliver the car to you in two weeks.

Monsieur Ibrahim   In two weeks? Impossible. I'll be dead in two weeks!

Moses   Two days later, they delivered the car outside the grocery shop.

Whilee he and **Monsieur Ibrahim** *create the car:*

Monsieur Ibrahim climbed inside and delicately touched all the controls with his long, slender fingers. Then he wiped his forehead and his face turned green.

Monsieur Ibrahim   I've forgotten, Momo.

Moses   But you did learn, didn't you?

Monsieur Ibrahim   Yes, a long time ago. My friend Abdullah taught me. But . . .

Moses   Yes?

Monsieur Ibrahim (*looking like a lemon*)   But cars were different then.

Moses   Were the cars you learned to drive pulled by horses, by any chance?

Monsieur Ibrahim   By donkeys, little Momo, by donkeys.

Moses   And what about your driving licence the other day? What was that?

Monsieur Ibrahim   Hmmm . . . an old letter from my friend Abdullah, explaining how his grape-picking went.

Moses   Well, looks like we're in deep shit!

Monsieur Ibrahim   That's for sure, Momo.

Moses   What about your Qur'an? Can't you find anything in there to give us a solution as you always do?

Monsieur Ibrahim   Of course not, Momo. They travel by camel in the Qur'an! So you can forget about driving tips . . . and the Qur'an isn't a manual for mechanics, it's for all things spiritual.

Moses   You could take driving lessons.

Monsieur Ibrahim   Never!

Moses (*as he takes a seat in the back of the car*)   As I wasn't old enough, Monsieur Ibrahim was the one who officially learned, while I was sitting in the back, not losing a word of what the instructor was saying. As soon as the lesson ended, we'd take our car and I'd sit behind the wheel. (*They squeeze past each other in the car to change seats.*) My driving was getting better and better.

Moses   Finally the summer came and we set off. We travelled all across Europe, to the Middle East, with our windows open. The universe got incredibly interesting when travelling with Monsieur Ibrahim. As I could only look at the road, he spent hours describing the landscapes, the sky, the clouds, the villages, the inhabitants. During that trip, I didn't see any of Europe. I heard it.

Until we stopped. Then, I smelled it.

Monsieur Ibrahim *murmurs, gets to audible level by the end of* **Moses'** *text – descriptions of the landscape, exclamations, surprising comments followed by wicked remarks.*

Monsieur Ibrahim   Ok, close your eyes, Momo. What kind of building are we in? Let's see if you can smell the religion. Take a deep breath.

Moses (*smells*)   I can smell candles. Catholic.

Monsieur Ibrahim   Well done. It's St Antony's.

Moses (*smells*)   I can smell incense – Orthodox.

Monsieur Ibrahim   Well done. It's the Hagia Sophia.

Moses (*smells*)   And here, I can smell feet. Quite smelly, actually.

Monsieur Ibrahim   Now, really, Momo! This is the Blue Mosque! A place which smells of human beings isn't good enough for you? Don't your feet ever smell? For me, this scent of socks in a place of prayer has something calming about it. It tells me I'm no better than my neighbour. I smell myself, I smell my fellow men, and I feel immediately better!

Moses   From Istanbul onwards, Monsieur Ibrahim talked less. He was moved. We were nearing his land.

Monsieur Ibrahim *and* **Moses** *enjoy a sunset.*

Monsieur Ibrahim   Soon, we're going to meet the sea I come from. I'm happy. You're with me, and I know what's in my Qur'an. Let's drive more slowly, Momo. I've always taken time over things. I've worked hard all my life, but at a slow pace. Doing things slowly is the key to happiness.

Moses   Where's that sea you come from? Will you show me on the map?

Monsieur Ibrahim   Don't bother me with maps, Momo. This isn't school! Look, what a beautiful mountain village this is. Stop here, I want to take you dancing.

Moses   Dancing?!

Monsieur Ibrahim   Absolutely, yes. 'Man's heart is locked up in a cage.' If you dance, your heart sings like a bird, and its song may reach God. Let's go to the tekke.

Moses   The what?

He took me to a tekke.

They enter, stand at the door, look around.

Moses   Funny kind of dance hall!

Monsieur Ibrahim   This isn't a dance hall, this is a monastery.

Music.

Moses   And that's the first time I saw the men whirling. The dervishes were wearing great robes of pale, flowing material. They were whirling and whirling.

Monsieur Ibrahim   You see, Momo, they're praying.

Moses   You call that praying?

Monsieur Ibrahim (*starting to turn*)   Try it, Momo, try it. Follow me.

Moses *copies* **Monsieur Ibrahim***'s movements. They whirl.*

Moses (*whirling*)   I'm happy being with Monsieur Ibrahim. (*Whirling.*) I'm no longer angry with my father for leaving.

Monsieur Ibrahim *breaks out of the rhythm, has to lean against something to catch his breath.*

Monsieur Ibrahim (*panting*)   So, Momo, did you think beautiful things?

Moses   Yes, it was incredible! I wasn't so angry at my father any more. And I think if I hadn't stopped I might have dealt with my mother.

Monsieur Ibrahim   You see, going to the tekke is a necessary thing. You get rid of bad thoughts. Better. You cleanse yourself.

Moses   But the soles of my feet are on fire from whirling so much. Next time I go praying, I'll wear different shoes.

Moses   From then on, we'd stop in a tekke almost every day. Sometimes, Monsieur Ibrahim wouldn't whirl. He'd only sip some tea and half-close his eyes. I'd whirl like crazy. No, in fact, I'd whirl to become less and less crazy.

Moses Then came the day that should never have happened. Monsieur Ibrahim told me that it was just a matter of hours before we'd get to his birthplace. He wanted to get there alone first, on reconnaissance. He asked me to wait for him under an olive tree.

The car smashed into a farm wall. I found him lying on the ground badly injured and bruised.

Moses   Monsieur Ibrahim!

Monsieur Ibrahim   This is where the journey ends, Momo.

Moses (*crying*)   I'm scared for you!

Monsieur Ibrahim   Well I'm not scared. I know what's in my Qur'an.

Moses   Monsieur Ibrahim!

Monsieur Ibrahim   I'm not dying, Momo. I'm joining the boundless.

Moses   That's my story. When I got back to Paris, I found out Monsieur Ibrahim had thought of everything. I inherited his money, his grocery shop and his Qur'an.

He opens the grey envelope and delicately removes the old book.

At last I was going to see what was in his Qur'an.

There were two dried-up flowers and a letter from his friend Abdullah.

Moses   And now I'm Momo, the guy who manages the grocery shop on the rue Bleue.

To everyone, I'm the street's Arab. Arab means open at night and on Sundays in the grocery business.

9 780413 775900